Walter Armstrong

Wrestling

With numerous illustrations

Walter Armstrong

Wrestling
With numerous illustrations

ISBN/EAN: 9783743323438

Manufactured in Europe, USA, Canada, Australia, Japa

Cover: Foto ©Andreas Hilbeck / pixelio.de

Manufactured and distributed by brebook publishing software
(www.brebook.com)

Walter Armstrong

Wrestling

BY

WALTER ARMSTRONG,

("CROSS-BUTTOCKER")

LATE HONORARY SECRETARY TO THE CUMBERLAND AND
WESTMORLAND WRESTLING SOCIETY IN LONDON,
AUTHOR OF "WRESTLIANA," ETC.

WITH NUMEROUS ILLUSTRATIONS.

NEW YORK:

FREDERICK A. STOKES COMPANY.

MDCCCXC.

CONTENTS.

The larger illustrations have been reproduced by Messrs. Waterlow, from photographs taken from Messrs. Jack Wannop and T. Thompson.

LIST OF ILLUSTRATIONS.

INTRODUCTION.

WRESTLING, though generally described by its exponents and admirers as an ancient English exercise, has claims far beyond this on history. So far as we can ascertain, it was the first form of athletic pastime, man's chief desire having been, from the beginning of the world, to get his fellow down—and too often to keep him there. Not only is a wrestling match to be found recorded in Holy Writ, but many of the earliest painters and sculptors with a taste for scriptural subject have made the combat between Michael and Lucifer a match at "fair holds" the latter coming to grief, generally by the "back-heel," the "click," or the "hipe," as the fancy or taste of the artist dictated.

When Greece, emerging from obscurity and ignorance, began to take the lead in civilization, in military knowledge, and in the cultivation of learning and sciences, the utility of public games, not only to infuse a generous and martial spirit into the minds of the young men, but also to increase their bodily strength, was too apparent to be neglected. Accordingly, we find that wrestling and other athletic exercises were not only practised in each particular state, but that the highest honours and rewards were bestowed on the victors at the Olympic, Nemean, and other games, where prizes were awarded and contended for before the whole nation. Without doubt, wrestling, beyond almost any other exercise, gives strength and firmness, combined with quickness and pliability to the limbs, vigour to the body, coolness and discrimination to the head, and elasticity to the temper, the whole forming an energetic combination of the greatest power to be found in man.

The influence of athletic sports in advancing Greece from a few petty states into the most powerful kingdom at that time in the world is universally acknowledged by all historians and commentators who have ever dealt with the subject. It is singular, however, to remark that while the fact is admitted by all modern legislators, few, or none, have recommended an imitation of the manly games referred to. Extracts could be selected from ancient history to prove the estimation in which this and other athletic exercises were held from the earliest period; but in this brief commentary it will be sufficient if we confine ourselves to a more recent date.

We are told that in the celebrated interview between Henry the Eighth of England and the French King Francis, which almost vied in magnificence and splendour with any spectacle of modern times, wrestling was deemed the most manly and entertaining amusement then exhibited in the presence of those two mighty monarchs and their courts. A great, and what would at the present day be called an international, display took place between a number of champions selected from both nations, in which our countrymen were victorious. However, one mortified French historian pretends their king left better wrestlers at home, and asserts that Francis himself was a most excellent wrestler, and in a contest between the two rival monarchs threw Henry with great violence. There is a certain amount of French gasconade as to the issue of the contest easily observable. If Henry was silly enough, out of courtesy to

Francis, to compete according to French rules, his defeat is easily understood, as the Gallic style of wrestling is the most absurd of all known systems.

Sir Walter Scott, in the fifth canto of "The Lady of the Lake," gives the following account of a wrestling match in the presence of the romantic King James, of Flodden memory :—

> " Now clear the ring, for hand to hand
> The manly wrestlers take their stand.
> Two o'er the rest superior rose,
> And proud demanded mightier foes ;
> Nor called in vain : for Douglas came ;
> For life is Hugh of Lambert lame ;
> Scarce better John of Alloa's fare,
> Whom senseless home his comrades bare.
> Prize of the wrestling match, the King
> To Douglas gave the golden ring."

This encounter was evidently on the catch-hold principle, as the words " hand to hand " give ample testimony that such was the system under which the champions competed. Again, in "The Antiquary," Sir Walter gives but a lame account of the encounter between Bothwell and Burley— "In the first struggle, the trooper seemed to have some advantage, and also in the second, though neither could be considered as decisive. In the third close, the countryman lifted his opponent fairly from the floor, and hurled him to the ground with such violence, that he lay for an instant stunned and motionless."

The celebrated James Hogg, the Ettrick Shepherd, has also introduced wrestling into his tales ; but, as Hogg himself, when he stripped for the fray, was in the habit of wrestling in top-boots, he scarcely can be quoted as an authority on this ancient and intricate pastime. Professor Wilson, again, was passionately fond of wrestling, and while he resided at Elleray, in Westmorland, gave a prize to be wrestled for annually at Ambleside, in the shape of five guineas and a silver-mounted belt to be given to the victor. Previous to the period alluded to, the usual prize in Cumberland and Westmorland had dwindled down to a leather strap, commonly called a belt, scarcely ever exceeding two shillings in value. Wilson was a proficient in athletic exercises, particularly in boxing, leaping, and walking; but he never entered the wrestling arena to compete for a prize, probably because his antagonists were not of equal rank. The grand old professor, however, at the close of the sports, which he frequently attended in various parts of Cumberland and Westmorland, would often try a fall with the winner, occasionally having the best of the encounters.

Without entering into any lengthened details, it should be observed that, ever since its institution, the modes of wrestling have been as various as they are at this time in England, America, and the Colonies. Back-hold wrestling still holds its own in Cumberland and Westmorland, and remains as popular as it was over a century ago. In Lancashire and the north of Ireland, the catch-hold or catch-as-catch-can system still finds favour; and in Devon and Cornwall, wrestling in canvas jackets continues to be the popular style, with certain modifications relative to kicking, formerly practised more especially by the Devonian exponents of the art. In the United States and Australia, the catch-hold system, which often includes ground wrestling, is the most fashionable; while in France, Germany, Switzerland, and Japan, a sort of catch-hold style has been adopted, subject to certain restrictions, to be hereafter commented upon. Of all known methods, however, the arms round the body, as practised in Cumberland and Westmorland and the Border counties, is, we consider, the best calculated to produce a display of dexterity and science.

Of course, many persons who understand little of the art generally, especially those blindly prejudiced in favour of that particular system which they are most familiar with, will cavil at this assertion. It may, however, be mentioned that those north-country wrestlers who took to catch-hold wrestling, for instance, George Steadman, the champion, John Wannop, John Graham, and others, threw all comers at their own game. In 1870, after Jameson and Wright had been completely foiled by the French champions, Le Bœuf and Dubois, at the Agricultural Hall, Steadman met the Gallic heroes at the Alexandra Palace and other places, and completely turned the tables on the burly and unwieldly giants. Steadman was especially bitter against Dubois, and on several occasions threw him and held the great hillock of flesh down the required time, in spite of all the resistance the infuriated Frenchman could make.

Ground wrestling, however, which means, if it means anything, simply a kind of dog-fight on the ground, is utterly opposed to our notions of sport, and can never find favour in this country; indeed, Lancashire is the only county in England where it is practised. The two shoulders on the ground and one hip, or two hips and one shoulder, generally described as "three points," which is the Devon and Cornwall definition of a fall, is somewhat more reasonable; yet the dissatisfaction these conditions frequently give rise to when a decision has to be given in a close fall is sometimes vexatious in the extreme, the result in many cases culminating in a wrangle; whereas, in the Cumberland and Westmorland fashion, if a wrestler touches the ground with any part of his body, his feet of course excepted, or when a man is thrown to the ground and his opponent falls plump on top of him, the merest tyro can then decide as to whom the verdict should go.

In the counties of Cumberland, Westmorland, Northumberland, and Durham, the sport still retains its prestige, and amounts in prizes are now given which would astonish our forefathers.

A thorough knowledge of any wrestling can be gained by practice alone, and that too should be commenced in early boyhood. It is very rare that a wrestler rises to eminence in the art whose start was made after getting well through his teens. In the north, it is part of almost every youth's education ; and frequently a youngster's wrestling celebrity at school clings to him through life, and often enables him more sturdily to fight the world's battle. None but those who have attended such wrestling rings as Carlisle or Grasmere can realize with what enthusiasm the sport is regarded in the Border counties, and although at most of the northern meetings horse-racing forms part of the amusements, the principal body of the spectators are present to see the wrestling, and that alone.

Even at Carlisle, which is now a considerable race meeting, the wrestling is the principal source of attraction, and commands the largest following. On the morning of the meeting, the many thousands who are seen flocking to the scene of action sufficiently testify to the interest excited, without any other inducement, and wherever a few canny country farmers are found conversing, such a remark as the following may be overheard. "O, aw care nowt aboot t' racing, aw's here to see t' rustlin', and nowt else." Probably the speaker has a strapping son who intends making his bow for the first time to a Cumbrian gathering. When such is the case, the interest is of course tenfold.

In Cumberland, wrestling most unmistakably runs in families, frequently through several generations, yet, strange to say, in only one case have a father and son won the heavy-weight prize in the Carlisle ring, viz. John Blair, of Solport Mill, in 1835, and William Blair, in 1883. It may therefore be argued that the taste for wrestling is inherited from the mother's side, as also the ability to achieve renown in the arena. Indeed, the Carlisle ring especially, is always favoured by a large contingent of the fair sex, who display a knowledge of the business in hand and an amount of enthusiasm simply incomprehensible to the uninitiated spectator, who, if he be a southerner, is perfectly bewildered by the strange dialect which greets his astonished ear.

While speaking of Cumberland and Westmorland wrestling, it is much to be regretted that the old society, which was established over a century ago, and was the oldest athletic club in London, should have suddenly collapsed without any apparent cause. It is a subject of congratulation, however, that under the auspices of a number of north-countrymen, headed by Professor Atkinson, F.R.C.V.S., of the Animal's Institute, the eminent bone-setter, a new society should so spontaneously have sprung up like a phœnix from the ashes of its predecessor, the ever-memorable Cumberland and Westmorland Society in London.

Years ago, an amateur wrestling society was suggested in the columns of two daily sporting journals by a gentlemen well-known in wrestling circles, but the idea was unsupported, and the proposition was abandoned. But when the new association became an accomplished fact, it seemed astonishing to many that the movement had not been set afoot long before. Through the equivocal conduct of many of the professional wrestlers, the old institution had at last to be bolstered up by running matches, as the public had begun to wake up to the knowledge that the wrestling contests by the brawny heroes of the north, as they were called, were often the hollowest of shams. Finally, when the old society ceased to exist, most of the balance in hand was given to the Cumberland Benevolent Institution and the Westmorland Society's Schools.   Under the new order of things, north-country wrestling may now be witnessed annually in London in all its native purity, and as the young club includes nearly one hundred effective wrestling members, it may be fairly assumed that the sport will flourish in the metropolis and hold its own with the numerous athletic bodies now in existence.

In 1871, the late Mr. J. G. Chambers, of aquatic and pedestrian celebrity, and some time editor of *Land and Water*, endeavoured to introduce and promote a new system of wrestling at the Lillie Bridge Grounds, West Brompton, which he denominated, " The Catch-as-catch-can Style; first down to lose."   Unfortunately, the new idea met with little support at the time, and a few years afterwards Mr. Chambers was induced to adopt the objectionable fashion of allowing the competitors to wrestle on all-fours on the ground.   This new departure was the forerunner of the total abolition of the sport at that athletic resort, and within a short period the wrestling, as an item in the programme there, was entirely wiped out.

Various other promoters of this exercise, notably Mr. J. Wannop, of New Cross, have attempted to bring the new system prominently before the public, with the view of amalgamating the three English styles, viz. the Cumberland and Westmorland, Cornwall and Devon, and Lancashire. Very little success, however, has attended their efforts, and it was thought by many well-wishers and patrons of the sport that the catch-hold idea would have to be abandoned. The sudden development, however, of the Cumberland and Westmorland Amateur Wrestling Society, brought the new style again prominently to the front, and special prizes were given for competition in that class at the Society's first annual midsummer gathering at the Paddington Recreation Grounds, which was attended by Lord Mayor Whitehead and sheriffs in state.

Wrestling on the "first down to lose" principle was new to many of the spectators, but it was generally approved of as a great step in advance of the loose-hold system, which includes struggling on the ground and sundry objectionable tactics, such as catching hold of the legs, twisting arms, dislocating fingers, and other items of attack and defence peculiar to Lancashire wrestling.

Certainly all impartial lovers of the sport must admit that it possesses a great advantage over those modes of wrestling which permit a man to throw himself on the ground, when he feels himself in danger of coming to grief by being placed on his back. Should this system come into universal practice, there is no reason why it should not become as popular as the Cumberland and Westmorland fashion, which has won its way to a front position among athletic exercises by the simplicity of its rules and its manly surroundings.

WRESTLING.

CHAPTER I.

CUMBERLAND AND WESTMORLAND STYLES.

THE northern school is, in our opinion, the proper one to graduate in, as it is evident, if two men are able to keep their equilibrium with their arms confined in the manner demanded by the hold in this style, they necessarily secure a great advantage with that restriction removed, *i.e.*, if they were allowed to unclasp their hands at will. It is an acknowledged fact that wrestlers who are proficient in the Cumberland and Westmorland style can readily adopt and rapidly become experts in any other, while the converse of this cannot be maintained.

The wrestlers are usually dressed in well-fitting and becoming costumes, and any lady may witness their competitions without her sense of delicacy being wounded in the least degree. Beyond all this, the northern style is freer from danger than any other known system; indeed, during the writer's forty years' experience, he cannot call to mind a single instance where a competitor has been hurt in a contest.

B

THE RULES.

On taking hold, the wrestlers stand up chest to chest, each placing his chin on his opponent's right shoulder, and grasping him round the body, each placing his left arm above the right of his antagonist.

When both men have got hold, and are fairly on their guard, the play commences, and, with the exception of kicking, they are allowed to use every legitimate means to throw each other.

If either party breaks his hold, that is, loses his grip, though not on the ground, and the other still retains his hold, the one so leaving loose shall be the loser.

If either man touches the ground with one knee only, or any other part of his body, though he may still retain his hold, he shall not be allowed to recover himself, but shall be deemed the loser.

If both fall to the ground, the man who is first down or falls under the other shall be the loser; but if they fall side by side, or otherwise, so that the umpires cannot decide which was first on the ground, it shall be what is technically termed a " dog fall," and shall be wrestled over again.

THE HOLD.

Opinions respecting the best methods of taking hold are various. Every wrestler, however, knows that the subject is a most difficult one, and a frequent source of dispute in the wrestling arena. On taking hold, the men stand chest to chest, as stated in the rules; but if a wrestler is bent on securing an unfair grip, he will, as a rule, lean to the left side, and by pinning his opponent's right arm close to the elbow cause him endless trouble, unless the umpires step in to the rescue and compel the offending party to stand squarely in front of his antagonist. Many wrestlers are fond of leaning to the left side when taking hold; but although such an awkward mode of standing will sometimes harass an adversary, it is frequently the cause of the other's downfall, as it is evident that leaning to either side must lay the wrestler open to attack, as he will necessarily be somewhat off his balance, whereas, by standing squarely, a man's position is bound to be much firmer and better adapted both for attack and defence.

Some wrestlers lean to the left so much that they lay themselves open to the cross-buttock in a remarkable degree, and when in the grip of an expert, frequently come to grief by that formidable chip. An advantageous hold to begin with is often half the battle in a contest, and considerable practice will render a man very dexterous in securing a telling grip at the proper time, *i.e.* when his opponent is standing in an insecure position. Many first-rate wrestlers differ as much in their notions of taking hold as in their methods of attack and defence. Thus, Edward Norman, the fourteen-stone Carlisle champion, is easily satisfied, and stands almost erect; while his rival, Hexham Clarke, of Seaton, in Cumberland, prefers a low hold; and the accomplished Thomas Kennedy, of Egremont, especially when he is aiming for the buttock, takes a slack hold. Other wrestlers, too, have a method of taking an easy grip, and mending it in a smart jerk after they clutch. This move very often throws an opponent off his guard and results in his defeat, because it will often occur that he soon finds himself with the worst hold of the pair.

Having secured a good grasp, it is always well to make play at once while the grip is retained, as a sudden move on the part of an opponent will often reverse the positions of the men ; but a skilful wrestler will be always very careful to keep his right arm well up, so as to prevent his opponent getting a low hold of him. If, however, he does not succeed in this, one equally skilled will inevitably gain an advantage, and thus the victory often rests with the party who possesses the best grip.

With regard to clasping the hands round the back of an opponent, the best way is to make the hands a couple of hooks, by placing all the fingers of one hand into the other hand held in the same way, so that the back of the right hand shall press on the small of the antagonist's back. Some men take hold with the right hand the other way, which does not give anything like such a good grip, as the right arm being under the left lends more purchase to it when the knuckles are pressed against the ribs. Laying hold of one wrist with the other hand, and clasping hands, are now out of fashion. The former method shortens the arms, and the latter gives an insecure grip.

THE BACK-HEEL.

When one wrestler gets a leg behind his opponent's heel on the outside, it is called back-heeling. This is one of the most useful throws in the whole series, and probably oftener used, and altogether a safer mode of flooring. an opponent than any other of the numerous methods with which wrestlers are conversant. It is also a saving measure, and when a wrestler is in danger of being lifted from the ground or swung, the insertion of the back-heel frequently brings about the downfall of an antagonist, especially if it be plied as near the ankle and as quickly as possible.

Directly a wrestler feels he is being back-heeled, he should slacken his hold and lean forward; if once he allows himself to be pushed back, over he must go. A slow and inexpert back-heeler can be hiped (see p. 13) with the back-heel in. This is frequently done by good hipers, who sometimes give the right leg, to invite a click, when a splendid fall is often the result. A long-legged man is always a dangerous customer with the back-heel. The best way to foil an opponent of this kind is to employ the hank (see p. 7), that is, if a wrestler feels himself going backwards, by keeping the back-heel in and turning in his side he may frequently twist his opponent under before reaching the ground.

There was, about the beginning of this century, an old-fashioned style of back-heel, called hamming. It consisted of the heel of the assailant being rapidly placed behind his opponent's knee. It was, however, a very clumsy move, and is never used at the present day, since so many new methods have cropped up undreamt of when the century was young. Those learning wrestling in the Cumberland and Westmorland style should commence their study of the art by getting proficient in the back-heel before attempting anything else. It is by far the easiest and safest method of going to work, and will be of more service to the young beginner than such unreliable chips as the·buttock, cross-buttock, or hipe, all of which, however, are very useful when practised by a proficient in the art. Always back-heel your opponent's right leg with your left; it is much safer than back-heeling his left leg with your right, as he cannot put in the *hank* so readily with the right leg.

THE HANK.

This is one of the most dangerous throws of all, and very difficult to stop when once firmly inserted; besides, it is one of the most artful and insidious chips in the whole calendar, and has made more men unexpectedly bite the dust than any other known method. When a cunning wrestler intends playing the hank, it is usual to see him stand in a rather sidelong position to begin with, when, immediately the hold is obtained, quick as thought, he whirls his left side to his opponent, clicks his right leg with his left on the inside, and pulls him backward, generally falling on him with all his weight. The only way to stop the hank is to lean forward, obtain a better hold, and hitch the aggressor over. Should the defendant allow himself to be pulled backward, scarcely anything can save him from being very heavily thrown. In the case of a novice, until he reaches the ground with an unpleasant thud, he is, as a rule, under the impression that he is having the best of the struggle. The "Druid" tell us, in "Saddle and Sirloin," that this somewhat unscientific chip was invented by the Fellside champion, James Elliot, of Cumrew, in Cumberland, about the year 1835, but it never found favour with the talent. "In fact," says this celebrated sporting writer, "a man is generally beaten when he puts it in, and,

THE HANK.

when it comes to a hug, he loses four falls out of five through it." Now we beg leave to differ from the "Druid" in the most emphatic manner. A lengthened experience in the wrestling arenas of the north proves the exact contrary, as in all the first-class rings in Cumberland and Westmorland during the last forty years, an expert hanker has rarely been known to get the worst of the throw, especially if he made up his mind to use the chip at the commencement of the struggle.

THE OUTSIDE CLICK.

This click is neither more nor less than a back-heel ; the latter, however, being an aggressive move, while the outside click is only used when the wrestler is on the defensive, it requires some mention. Without its aid, many of our light-weight wrestlers would never have been heard of, especially when pitted against their heavier rivals. Of course, every one knows that a tall, heavy man ought to be able to lift a lighter one, four or five inches less in stature, clean off his legs with such a purchase as the north-country hold supplies; but how often has it happened that the smaller wrestler, in order to prevent his being lifted from the ground, has clicked his gigantic adversary on to his head or flat on his back, and thus immortalized himself? The most expert light-weight would have no earthly chance with a moderate heavy-weight were it not for the outside click, which should be plied directly he feels himself leaving his mother soil. Again, many a big man in swinging a lighter opponent has found himself on his head, while all the time he was under the impression that he was "burying" the "laal 'un." Light-weight men cannot attach too much importance to this invaluable chip, as it occasionally happens that the click on the outside is the only defence they can make against superior weight and strength. In the suddenness of the action consists its efficacy when the assailant is busy with some move by which he intends to finish the contest "right off the reel."

THE INSIDE CLICK.

To become a proficient at the inside click requires an enormous amount of practice; but when the exponent obtains a thorough mastery over its intricacies he is a dangerous customer. It is carried out in the same manner as the hank, with this exception, that when the assailant inside clicks his man with the right or left leg, he does not turn his side, but keeps facing him squarely.

The best way to insert the inside click is to jerk your opponent forward, when he is almost compelled to make at least one step. He then naturally attempts to steady himself, and hangs back; this of course assists the adroit inside clicker, who dashes in the chip, adding to it all the weight at his command. To carry out the inside click successfully, a tight hold is absolutely necessary.

Hard falls often result when the chip is effectually applied in the course of a struggle, as the unfortunate party who knocks under seldom expects such a sudden downfall. A false move on the part of the wrestler who places either his right or left leg too near his opponent's supplies the opportunity for an adept at the inside click, who, quick as a flash of electricity, has his man firmly and squarely on his back, and not unfrequently on his head as a preliminary. The cross click is not by any means such a formidable

stroke as the other, as in standing in front of an opponent, his right leg has to be clicked with your right and his left with your left. Both are exceedingly dangerous to the defendant ; but in the inside click the man who plies the chip runs little risk, because, even if he fails, he secures a better hold and gets into a good position for using either the right or left leg hipe or the cross-buttock. It is unlike the back-heel, a failure in which generally results in defeat, as the antagonist obtains a better hold, and has his man at his mercy. The back-heel once inserted should be determinedly persevered in, unless the buttock or hipe can be brought into operation, which seldom happens when the unfortunate back-heeler has got into difficulties.

The Cross-buttock.

For this throw, you turn your left side to your opponent, get your hip partially underneath him, then, quick as lightning, cross both his legs by your left and lift him from the ground. Both will come down, but your assailant will be undermost.

A man skilled in this method of wrestling usually strives for a loose hold, as such gives him more room to make play and get under his opponent. The left cross-buttock is the best, as it is easier plied than the right. Great rapidity of action is necessary, as if the least hitch or delay occurs, the assailant's position is fraught with danger.

The arms, when the attack is made, should be kept tightly round the opponent's neck or shoulders, as, unless the effort is seconded by the arms and upper part of the body, the act of throwing the leg across would be a fatal movement on the part of the assailant. It sometimes happens that by turning in the left side quickly, with very slack holds, you get into a position exactly in front of your opponent. In that case, it is necessary to keep the hands fast and strike across both legs as quickly as possible, while at the same time your adversary should be twisted forwards with all the

THE CROSS-BUTTOCK.

power at your command. If properly done, the result will be satisfactory; but the slightest bungle in the movement places the aggressor completely in the hands of his

adversary, as all he has to do in most cases is to lift his
man up and throw him over his right knee on to his back, or
he may, by getting fairly behind him and putting one leg or
foot across both of the defendant's, treat the unfortunate
cross-buttocker to what is in some places called "grandy-
stepping." The cross-buttock is a very fancy-looking move ;
it is not at all dangerous, and easy falls nearly always result
therefrom, although to the uninitiated they look extremely
perilous.

The Buttock.

This differs from the previous fall, in that you get your
hip further under the adversary and throw him right over
your back. Beyond all question, the buttock, when successfully performed, takes the palm as the spiciest of all
wrestling chips ; but it is a more unsafe move even than the
cross-buttock, and requires also greater strength and art than
the other manœuvre. To turn your back quickly round to
your opponent and shoot him up in the air over your head is
a feat of no ordinary difficulty (see p. 13). The number of
famous buttockers in the present day could be counted on
the fingers of one hand. It looks very well in exhibition
wrestling, but is seldom now resorted to in arenas where
fair contests are insisted upon. When the assailant, by
turning in quickly with very loose holds, gets exactly before
and with his back to his opponent, by keeping his hands
fast, does not throw his opponent over his head, his position
is almost a hopeless one, as the defendant will secure a
telling hold and throw him in the same way as a miss would
lose him the fall in the cross-buttock. Buttocking is little
known beyond the confines of Cumberland and Westmorland, as no other style of wrestling is so suitable for its
display.

THE HIPE.

The hipe may be made with either leg. The left-leg hipe, which is here figured, has been much practised during

THE BUTTOCK.

recent years; but in our opinion it is inferior as an aggressive move to the right leg. It may be thus described. Lift your opponent and carry him to the right, at the same time striking the inside of his right thigh with your left knee, then, by lifting your left leg as high as you can, you will be enabled to place your man on his back without allowing him to touch the ground with his feet. In the right hipe, as the right arm is under your opponent's left, he can be lifted much higher than in the left, where, the left arm being over the opponent's right, he cannot be lifted with the same purchase. The left-leg hipe has, however, several points to recommend it, as, should it fail, the man operating is in a fair position for the inside click and the cross-buttock. The best way to stop the hipe is either to apply the click very low down, or close the knees, and by turning sideways the assailant will be completely foiled, and must set you down again. If possible, however, endeavour to keep on the ground in the first instance, and your position will be safe enough, as both the inside and outside clicks come in quite naturally after an unsuccessful attempt at hipeing.

A tall wrestler who is an expert hiper is always a terror to a man of smaller stature. Edward Norman, of Carlisle, who stands close on six feet, is at present the best hiper in England. He hipes with either leg, and if he misses with the one, the other is soon plied with fatal effect. When hipeing was introduced to the north, some three-quarters of a century ago, it was little noticed at first; but when it was tried by Thomas Richardson, of Hesket, about the year *1814,*

and the celebrated William Wilson, of Ambleside, those two worthies soon found what a formidable weapon they had got hold of. Up to the present day it is probably the most prominent of all the north-country methods comprised in the science of fair "felling."

THE SWINGING HIPE.

The swinging hipe differs in no material degree from the hipe pure and simple, except that it is necessary for the wrestler to swing his antagonist after lifting him, and previous to applying the hipe. It is a very clever chip, and difficult to stop, as, when a man is swung off his legs, with no possible chance of clicking his opponent, he must naturally come to the ground, unless he possesses the agility of a cat. Occasionally a very able wrestler will land on his feet, and with the impetus given him will swing his adversary on to his back; but this rarely happens. The best swinging hiper within living memory was William Jackson, of Kennie-side, in Cumberland, who for a number of years was champion of England. Jackson, who was celebrated for his fairness in taking hold, frequently swung his man round a complete circle, and rarely fell on his opponent—a very remarkable feat, as it seldom happens that a wrestler can throw another without falling on him.

THE OUTSIDE STROKE.

There are few surer methods of "grassing" an opponent in the Cumberland and Westmorland fashion than the out-side stroke with the left leg. The best way to use this chip is to twist the defendant round to the left, and by striking him with the left foot against the outside of his right leg or ankle, with the assistance of the arms, he is very easily turned

over on to his back by an expert performer.   Another style,
now completely abandoned, was termed " in and out," owing
to striking out with the leg, so that the knee of the assailant
is outside his opponent's and the foot inside his ankle or

THE OUTSIDE STROKE.

small of the leg, placing a kind of lock upon the knee and
leg.   At the present day, it would be absolutely impossible
for any first-class wrestler to be thrown by this antiquated
move, although fifty years ago it was a fashionable chip.

Another way is effected by feinting at the opponent's right leg with your left leg, and crossing it with your right. This stroke requires great quickness and dexterity, and is, when well executed, one of the surest and best methods of wrestling practised. Few men, are, however, proficient in it. The right outside stroke is now seldom used, as it is well known among wrestlers that, in the case of failure in plying it, the antagonist at once secures a rasping hold, and generally becomes master of the situation, unless the cross-buttock can be used instanter. Norman, of Carlisle, is now the best outside striker in England, and uses both legs with equal facility, The Carlisle champion is almost without a rival as a scientific exponent of the art in which he excels.

THE BREAST STROKE.

This stroke was brought into notice about half a century ago by Mossop, of Egremont, who floored all the champions of the day with it on its first introduction. There is nothing particularly clever about the manœuvre ; the assailant has merely to grasp his man firmly, twist him suddenly to one side and as suddenly to the other ; but it requires great development of the chest in order to accomplish it successfully. It is very difficult to meet, and time after time has foiled the best men in England. In later years, the celebrated Richard Wright, of Longtown, was the best exponent of the chip, and often did great execution with it. When Wright, who was a burly, thick-set man, got the proper hold, it was all over with his opponent, who, as a rule, could not make out what he had been thrown by, as the legs are not brought into play, the whole performance being executed by the arms and chest.

c

The foregoing are the principal falls used by the best
Cumberland and Westmorland wrestlers of the day in such
arenas as Carlisle, Grasmere, Morpeth, Pooley Bridge, and,
indeed, wherever wrestlers meet in friendly rivalry in the
north of England and south of Scotland, where the ancient
pastime is becoming more popular year after year.

CHAPTER II.

CORNISH AND DEVONSHIRE STYLES.

UNLIKE the friendly rivalry which animates the genial race
of giants who hail from Cumberland and Westmorland, a
deadly feud has from time immemorial existed between the
counties of Cornwall and Devon. In the former county,
where this antagonistic feeling runs particularly high, a
north-country wrestler has been known to be welcomed with
open arms; whereas, among the rural population in the
wrestling districts, a Devonian has often been received with
a shower of brickbats.

Whether their kicking propensities have or have not
influenced and inflamed this hostility has never been tho-
roughly established. As kicking, however, was never fashionable in Cornwall, the fact of a Cornishman in an encounter
with a Devonian occasionally having a considerable area of
skin sliced from his shins by a pair of formidable shoes,
made of hard baked leather, supplemented by a piece of
sheet iron, may have something to do with the inveterate
quarrel between the wrestlers of the two counties.

The principal difference in their methods of wrestling
was that, in former times, kicking was practised in Devon,
but not in Cornwall. The Cornishmen, however, when they
ventured into the enemy's territory, were found to be not

much behind their rivals in the use of the boot, while their science has been considered superior to that of the Devonians. The two styles have now, however, been amalgamated, and the only dissimilarity that exists consists in the different system of going to work observable in wrestlers hailing from the different counties. Hugging and heaving were always the Cornishmen's characteristics ; whereas, the men of Devon, as has been observed before, relied more on their expertness in kicking and a dexterous use of the jacket, which is worn only for the purpose of wrestling.

THE COSTUME.

The west-country wrestlers, as they are called, do not adorn themselves in such picturesque costumes as the northern men, who are distinguished for their handsome-fitting tights. Certainly, at the present day, they take their shoes off, but rarely their trousers, which they tuck up, and, after stripping to the shirt, the jacket is donned. This is made of strong linen, and hangs on the wearer very loosely, as far down as his hips, and is tied at the front by two strings. The sleeves are also made loose, for the convenience of both parties in catching hold. There is a regulation length for

the strings, which are the same in all jackets, and in order to secure the garments being as open as possible, the strings are tied at the extreme ends, as this prevents the opponent taking that firm hold which he would inevitably obtain if the jacket were tighter.

Instead of writing down the names and drawing them together, as in Cumberland and Westmorland, the men who intend to compete challenge each other by throwing a hat into the ring, which is answered in the same manner.

Position.

The position before taking hold is not a very graceful one. With the feet wide apart, the knees slightly bent, the hands are held in front, and a sharp look-out is kept on the adversary, so as to find an opening for a hold.

Soon the men, however, assume a stooping attitude, and endeavour to grasp each other by the jackets. This is often a very tiresome business; but when they once get into hold the throw is soon over. As two shoulders and one hip on the ground constitute a fall, or two hips and one shoulder, or in a "four point" match two shoulders and two hips, it frequently happens that a "no fall" is the verdict. A man must be thrown fairly on his back on all the required "points" before any other portion of his body touches the ground ere the fall is gained. Ground wrestling, as in Lancashire, is forbidden, consequently a man must be thrown very decisively for the verdict to go against him, and an expert wrestler, when he feels himself going, adroitly makes for the ground face downwards, so that his opponent shall have no opportunity of landing him on his back.

The wrestlers are at liberty to alter their hold as often as they please; but the hold is subject to certain restrictions. No competitor is allowed to take hold of an opponent's drawers, handkerchief, or belt, or to take the two collars of his opponent's jacket in one hand for the purpose of strangling him; but he may grasp the bottom corners of his jacket, or he may slip his hand under the jacket behind his antagonist's back, and, by bringing it over the shoulder, grasp the opposite collar, and thus secure a telling hold. This hold is allowed in Cornwall, but not permitted in Devonshire; although the latter's ruling is usually adopted in contests by the best representatives of the two counties; but the same strictness in conducting wrestling gatherings and giving decisions in the case of

THE HOLD.

suspicious-looking back-falls which is the rule in Devonshire is not observable in Cornwall.

The " fair back-fall" difficulty has always been a most serious drawback to this style of wrestling, as no judge, however competent and firm, can give satisfaction to the partisans of the men when the conditions are such that an artful performer, although thrown, can often wriggle on to his side, if not absolutely held down, and claim to wrestle over again, and carry on the manœuvre till the time for adjournment arrives, or darkness sets in, when he can claim a draw, although having the worst of the encounter, simply because his opponent had failed to satisfy the judges that he had thrown his man on the requisite number of points, whereas, had the conditions been different—for instance, "first down to lose"—he would probably have stood no chance whatever.

Many an inferior west-country wrestler has become famous on account of his getting-down tactics who would never have been heard of under other rules, where the wreath of victory was given only to the man who stood on his legs, and not to the one who artfully foiled his adversary after reaching the ground. The catch-hold style of wrestling is easier learned than the northern back-hold fashion, and is a more natural system of going to work in an unexpected rough-and-tumble encounter; but the western style has this drawback—its exponents are almost helpless without the regulation jacket, whereas a man who can wrestle in the Cumberland and Westmorland mode can acquit himself fairly well in any other, as the very fact of having liberty to quit his hold and renew it without being disqualified gives him advantages he does not possess in his own style; besides, whenever a northern wrestler gets the Cumbrian grip on a west-country performer, the latter is almost certain to get a fair back-fall, as the hands being locked together, small chance exists of being able to avoid being thrown on three points, or probably four.

The two best holds are the "fore-hand play" and the "after-play." In the first you are almost in front of your opponent, whereas in the latter you are behind him.

The Fore-hand Play.

This is considered the best by experts in the exercise. To secure the hold for the fore-hand play, catch your antagonist by the right elbow or wrist, and hold fast by the jacket, at the same time seize him with the right hand by the bottom of his jacket, close above the hip-bone.

Directly these movements are executed, a firm hold must be kept, throw your weight forward, turn yourself round to the left, so as almost to get your back to your antagonist, thus you will have the fore-hand play, and he will have the after-play. Your adversary, if he is an expert, will possibly attempt to take the fore-hand play, by laying hold of your elbow and side at the same time that you take hold of his, and each will be attempting to turn his back at the same moment. In such a position, quickness, and a knowledge of the art, combined with weight and strength, will decide the issue.

The After-play.

To get into position for the after-play, seize your opponent's left collar with your right hand, and grasp him round the back as firmly as possible.

The best movements for the fore-hand play are the outside lock, the inside lock, the cross lock, the cross-heave, and the cross-buttock, and those for the after-play are the double lock, the heave, the cross-heave, the home tang, the outside-clamp, and the pull-under.

THE OUTSIDE LOCK.

After having turned your back to your adversary, throw your right leg over the outside of his right, and twist your foot round it so that your toe comes to the inside of his ankle, twist yourself to the left, keeping a tight hold the while, and, as you nearly lift him from the ground, he is almost certain to fall on his back, especially if you retain your grasp and keep the outside lock or click in the position in which it was first placed. If you fail to throw your opponent and keep on your own legs, it is unsafe to remove the lock, and often results in defeat.

In order to stop the outside lock, should the adversary's head be under your arm, he will resort to the inside clamp, by striking the inside of your left leg with the outside of his left foot, and, by pushing yours forward and twisting you round, may probably make you fall on your back. Should his head, however, be free, he will most likely ply the outside clamp, by throwing his left leg over your left thigh. If you are thrown backward, and both are coming to the ground, he will endeavour to turn himself so as to fall on his left side, in order that he may turn you on your back and shoulders. If the throw be forward, he may, by using the half-nelson (see p. 41), or by pressing the back of your neck with his left hand, throw you on your face.

THE INSIDE LOCK FORWARD.

This is both a forward and backward movement. After getting into holds for the inside lock, twist your right leg round the inside of your adversary's left, by inserting it between his legs after the style of the outside lock, and proceed on the same system, and if vou find vou cannot throw your antagonist, un-ship the lock, and play the cross-buttock, as you have your man in a grand position for the operation.

To stop the inside lock, the defendant will most probably pull all his might with his left arm round your waist, or press with his left hand against the back of your head, which manœuvre may bring you down.

The inside lock backward resembles the Cumberland and Westmorland hank. If you have a good grip, after twisting your right leg round your adversary's left, you may safely fall backward, and make sure of throwing your opponent, as the leverage supplied by the lock inside is certain to bring him on his back, very unpleasantly too, as the fact of the two wrestlers being glued together, as it were, causes them to fall as solidly as a single plank. The best method of stopping this formidable move is to play the double lock, which is brought about by the defendant throwing his right heel inside your left and pressing backward, or with the cross-heave, which is a capital defence against both the inside lock forward and the outside lock.

The Inside Lock Backward.

This is merely another illustration of the Cumbrian hank. After twisting your right leg round the inside of your opponent's left, turn quickly and forcibly to the right, when both will, as a rule, fall backward, and by keeping a firm grip your antagonist is almost bound to fall underneath, unless he presses your head forward with his hand as in the diagram. In that case, the best way is either to aim for the cross-buttock or a fresh grip, as so long as he keeps his hand on your head and retains a firm grasp by the collar of your jacket, you stand a poor chance of throwing him backward.

The Double Lock.

This is used as a defensive measure, and is found particularly useful when a wrestler is in danger of being lifted bodily from the ground. It is a very effective method, too, of stopping the outside lock and the inside lock forward. Directly you feel you are going to be lifted off your feet, twist your right heel round your opponent's left on the inside, at the same time throw your left leg over his right and make a back-heel of it; then, if you press your antagonist backward, you may possibly give him the cross-heave.

THE HEAVE.

In this fall, both parties are in the same position, and a considerable amount of science is often displayed in consequence. On facing your opponent, place your right arm round his right shoulder, and reach over to his left loin, so that you have him under your right arm, then slip the left hand under him, so as to get hold of his left elbow. This often makes a capital fall, the unfortunate one being frequently thrown a complete somersault. The greatest promptitude is necessary to stop the heave, and the cross-buttock is frequently brought into play as a defensive measure, or the cross lock, which is executed by putting the right heel inside the adversary's right heel as sharply as possible, at the same time sending him backward with a sudden jerk. It is performed after the manner of the Cumbrian inside cross click, and ought to be of more frequent use, as it is one of the best chips on the board. The only difference between the cross-buttock and the hip is this : the quick action of the legs is the principal factor in the former, whereas the hip is more nearly allied to the northern buttock.

The cross-heave from the after-play is accomplished by

passing your left hand round your opponent's back to his left loin, taking care that your elbow is not in his grasp.

Hold firmly with both hands, and lift your antagonist off the ground as high as you can, and, as you both come down together, turn yourself round to the left, and if you have retained your grip, he must of necessity fall on both his shoulders.

The HOME-TANG is effected by getting both hands round the chest to the left side. It is seldom, however, brought into play, and is easily stopped by the hip or buttock.

The INSIDE CLAMP and the OUTSIDE CLAMP, although defensive chips properly speaking, are often used as throws when a chance arises, and have been found useful in stopping the outside lock and other formidable manœuvres. The former is merely an inside click or lock under another name; while the latter is simply an outside lock, or back-heel, used as a means of defence under difficulties.

The PULL-UNDER is performed thus :—Pass your left hand under your opponent's chest to his left loin, and, by making him play the inside lock, you have him fixed to all intents and purposes.

It may be well to mention here, for the benefit of the uninitiated, that the Cumberland and Westmorland buttock and hank are precisely the same respectively as the Cornish and Devon fore-hip and back lock ; the Cumbrian buttock is the collar and elbow hip-lock; and the Cumbrian hank stands good for the collar and elbow grape-vine, the favourite chip of the famous American "strangler," Evan Lewis.

The principal objection that can be urged against the west-country style of wrestling is in regard to their definition of a fall. If ever the promoters could see their way to adopt the principle of "first down to lose," as the climax of a struggle, the system would be more popular all over the country; but the sport is surrounded and fettered by a host of unintelligible rules, which are simply intolerable, and seem to have been deliberately framed for the purpose of causing endless disputes. If such was the intention of the original authors, they have succeeded admirably, as the frequent bickerings at their gatherings have at last almost abolished the exercise in every part of the country except in the two counties from which it sprung. Such olden champions as Abraham Cann, Polkinhorne, Tom Cooper, W. Pollard, Chappell, Sam Rundle, and Jos Menear were a credit to their native districts. Certainly, many good wrestlers are to be found in both the counties at the present day, who without doubt are deserving of more patronage than they receive.

CHAPTER III.

LANCASHIRE STYLE.

THE Lancashire style of wrestling is, without doubt, the roughest and most uncultivated of the three recognized English systems, as it includes catching hold of the legs, wrestling on the ground, and other objectionable methods of attack and defence. In Lancashire, wrestling displays are confined to matches promoted by the proprietor of some popular pedestrian resort, and differ as much as it is possible to imagine from the immense gatherings in the arenas of Cumberland and Westmorland, where sometimes nearly two hundred wrestlers will assemble, varying in weight from nine stone up to twenty stone odd.

The Lancashire system is closely allied to the French style. The only material difference is that the French forbid tripping and catching hold of legs, whereas both are allowed in the County Palatine, in addition to the use of any *fair* means of throwing an antagonist. Dressed in light, airy costumes, usually a pair of bathing drawers and a pair of stockings, to prevent the feet from slipping, the wrestlers confront each other in the arena ready for action, and after numerous feints, both catch hold by the wrists and fall struggling to the ground. Here the real tussle begins, the point aimed at being to bring the antagonist on his back with both shoulders touching the ground at once, as that constitutes a fair back-fall, if the fallen one can be held down a few seconds, or long enough to satisfy the referee, who usually has anything but a rosy time of it while the scrimmage lasts.

A favourite trick is for one of the combatants to seize the other by the back of the head and send him heels over head, when it seems as if nothing could save him from falling on his back; with a desperate wriggle round, however, and an acrobatic leap, he often cleverly lands on his chest, and at once commences either to play his adversary a similar trick or to make a sudden and fresh attack. Sometimes a wrestler will apparently make an unsuccessful attempt to wrench off the other's head, twist his arms from the sockets, or break his fingers, finally rolling him bodily over, all of which are eluded in a simply marvellous manner. The elasticity of their movements is at times some-thing remarkable, as they struggle, writhe, and twist for hours together before obtaining a fall. Sometimes one will throw the other over on his back, and, suddenly getting uppermost, try to force down the shoulders, which only the head and heels support, the body forming a perfect arch. All in vain, the agile wrestler is sure to escape as if by magic, and come down on his chest, when a fearful struggle again ensues, until one or the other is tired out, and is finally compelled to allow his shoulders to be forced to the ground.

The struggle between two heavy-weights possesses a touch of the terrible. Although they pursue the same tactics as the light-weights, it is a source of amusement to the un-initiated spectator to see an eighteen-stone man spin lightly round on his head, come down like a feather on his chest, and regain his feet as actively as a cat, prepared to renew the struggle with redoubled energy. Stamina is a necessary factor in this class of wrestling, in conjunction with a perfect knowledge of the business. Frequently one man will lift the other up by the legs and keep him walking on his hands, and yet find it impossible to throw him ; and as this, and similar acrobatic movements are kept up often for hours before a match can be decided, the most rigid training is required for such an exhausting combat.

A brief glance at the rules relating to Lancashire wrestling will now be sufficient for all practical purposes. As has been previously stated, the wrestlers compete in their stocking feet, and are allowed to catch hold where they please, but they must not scratch, throttle, pull each other's ears, or attempt to maim each other by unfair practices. At the commencement of an encounter, the wrestlers face each other, and assume the same position as the Cornish and Devon men ; but there the resemblance between the two

styles ends, as the real struggle begins after the men are
on the ground.

In a Lancashire match, the office of referee is no sinecure,
yet a firm judge can often quell the partisanship of the most
turbulent votary of the sport by giving his decision without
hesitation. Fifteen minutes are allowed between the falls,
and the referee is invested with full power to decide any
point not provided for in the articles of agreement, subject
to no appeal in a court of law. When a match is not
concluded on the day appointed, the referee orders the
combatants to meet again and commence wrestling after
being weighed, at the same time and place every day (except
Sunday), until a decision is arrived at. The reweighing day
by day is a very sensible clause, as it prevents the man who
has had to reduce himself putting on flesh and thus securing
an advantage over his opponent when the men have agreed
to a certain weight. While the contest is proceeding, if the
wrestlers get beyond the boundary of the ring, the referee
must separate them, and place them in the position where
they left off.

With regard to the referee, should he prove either in-
competent or prejudiced, the manager of the grounds, or
those interested, can disqualify him and agree upon
another official. When a new referee has been appointed
during a contest, the wrestlers must commence afresh.
Throttling, although forbidden in the rules, is difficult to
prevent, and is often resorted to when the men are on the
ground. Although a distinct rule is laid down against
throttling, wrestlers are allowed to break fingers or arms
if they can satisfy the referee that such took place during a
fairly-conducted struggle for the mastery, and not through
any desire to deliberately act in an unfair manner. A strict
referee can often keep the men within the rules laid down

for their guidance, but a weak one has little power over the. competitors when their blood is up, and some glaring enormities are often perpetrated.

Among all the fantastic tricks played by Lancashire wrestlers, the "double nelson" bears the palm, and is the most dangerous. It is brought about by getting behind the antagonist, and placing both arms under his; the assailant then clasps his hands behind the neck of his opponent and bends his head downwards in such a manner that his breast-bone will give way if he does not previously measure his length on the ground. The move is, however, difficult to play, and is not often attempted, as many wrestlers have been thrown over their adversary's head, when they have failed to bring it off with a heavily built man.

Lancashire wrestlers are not famous for their proficiency in the art of tripping or for leg-throws, although experts in the Lancashire style know most of the chips used by catch-hold wrestlers generally. Their principal throws are catching hold of one leg with both hands, with the view of hoisting an opponent on to his head, the double nelson, the half-nelson, the heave, and the flying mare, the three last-named of which have been described elsewhere (see pp. 41, 27, 37). In a rough-and-tumble encounter, when "all is in," a knowledge of Lancashire wrestling might be of service; but even in a street fight it is not the fashion for an Englishman to battle on the ground, but to allow his opponent to get up again. The Lancashire system teaches the very reverse, and its exponents seldom commence operations in earnest until they either get down on their knees or on all fours; consequently the art of standing up has not been so much cultivated as the best method of getting down on the ground in a certain position.

D

CHAPTER IV.

CATCH-AS-CATCH-CAN STYLE.

EVERY one must admit that the catch-hold fashion is a most rational style of wrestling, as the competitors are not restricted by any rules as to taking and retaining a particular hold, but are at liberty to catch each other as they please, as in a natural struggle, provided they do not hold by the legs or clothes; in fact, catching hold lower than the waist is not allowed, and any portion of the body down constitutes a fall, as in the Cumberland and Westmorland style.

Now a word to beginners, under catch-as-catch-can rules. It may safely be said that the means of acquiring perfection in wrestling and boxing are the same, and we often find light weights comparatively the best in either exercise, and men about thirteen, or between thirteen and fourteen stone the acknowledged champions, because they are, as a rule, so much superior in science to very heavy men as to render a few stones in weight of no great importance. The principle upon which this fact is founded will be sufficiently clear to those who, not content with a superficial knowledge, wish to examine the source it springs from. To arrive at the top of the tree in either wrestling or boxing, a complete knowledge of the art, and varied and effective action are necessary, and neither of these requisites can possibly be acquired without continued practice with superiors, equals, and inferiors, both in respect of science and weight; and, in order to become a perfect master of the art, such practice is absolutely necessary. It is easy for light weights and not difficult for men of thirteen and fourteen stone to find opponents of their own build, but very rare for those above that weight to meet with equals or superiors willing to engage with them, and hence their deficiency in science and action. Thus it is almost impossible for a heavy man to acquire the science and action which often distinguish the middle and light weights in such an extraordinary degree.

The Attitude.

Before coming to close quarters, the wrestlers assume a similar position to that usually adopted by the Cornwall and Devon and Lancashire exponents of the art, excepting that they stand in a more upright attitude than the former, and generally aim either for a head-hold or a grip round the waist. The head-hold is considered the best by experts, as it supplies opportunities for the back-heel, the inside click, the outside stroke, the buttock, etc. The grasp round the waist, especially if the under-hold can be obtained by a wrestler who knows the Cumberland and Westmorland method, gives the fortunate possessor of the grip an immense advantage over his opponent, who can only clasp his man over the arms or round his neck; consequently the latter is almost bound to go down with a man about his own weight. Many of the modes of attack and defence are so similar to those which distinguish the Cumberland and Westmorland method, that we feel sure a careful perusal of the various chips mentioned at an earlier portion of this work will be beneficial to the amateur catch-hold wrestling aspirant.

All the throws already described, unless obviously opposed to the principles of the catch-hold style, apply equally to it with such modifications only as are necessitated by the differences in the holds. It will not be necessary therefore to describe them all again, but the following may be found useful :—

The Back-heel.

In every system of wrestling the back-heel comes into play, and it is not too much to say that the back-heel of any one style bears a striking resemblance to all the others. No matter how much a man may be ignorant of wrestling generally, he has a kind of undefined notion that the best way to throw an antagonist is to back-heel him. In the main this doctrine is pretty correct; at the same time, the back-heel is not without its risks to the aggressor if he does not know how to ply it. In catch-hold wrestling, the best way to use the back-heel is to catch your opponent round the .head, jerk him forward, and as he will naturally step in with one leg, place your foot behind his on the outside and bend him over backwards; if you have weight and strength enough, he is certain to go. The back-heel can be foiled by clasping your antagonist round the waist, with the under-hold if possible, when the hipe (see p. 13) will come into play; or by suddenly turning round sideways with your arms round your adversary's neck, the hank (see p. 7) can be applied. In attempting these movements, however, it is of the utmost importance that a firm hold should be retained, as a good performer is sometimes easily pushed down in this style of wrestling should he accidentally lose his grip of his opponent; whereas, under the Cumberland and Westmorland conditions, the fact of the hands being

firmly clasped together frequently keeps both competitors on their legs, and often prolongs the contest.

THE FLYING MARE.

This is a very effective throw, but requires great rapidity

THE FLYING MARE.

of execution, as upon that entirely depends its success. Seize your opponent's left wrist with your right hand, then, quick as thought, turn your back upon him, at the same time grasp his left elbow with your left hand, and swing him over your back, as in the buttock, with a sudden jerk. The best method of preventing this is, directly your opponent gets in front of you, click him in front and clasp him round the body with your right arm. By this means you may get in the front position, when the half-buttock should come into operation, and your antagonist will, as a rule, be thrown on his face. The flying mare more properly belongs to the Cornish and Devon system, but it has been thought advisable to introduce it here.

THE OUTSIDE STROKE.

This is a very useful manœuvre in catch-hold wrestling, providing you can induce your opponent to stand with one leg well advanced; for instance, the left one. Place your right hand on his left shoulder, at the same time strike, as in the northern style, close to the ground (not at the knee, as some *authorities* have recommended), and simultaneously seize him under his right arm-pit and twist him on to his back. Should your opponent, however, change legs, endeavour then to get a head hold (as in the diagram), and strike his right leg

in the same manner with your left. The safest way to elude either stroke is to stand square with both legs, and avoid giving your opponent any chance of throwing you off your guard. An expert outside striker sometimes only wants his opponent to stand with one leg well to the front, in order to be enabled to throw him on his back without · either closing or falling himself. In casual encounters this stroke is invaluable. In such, always strike with the right foot at your antagonist's left, at the same time give his left wrist, if you can, a slight jerk forward. The movement is usually so totally unexpected that most men will be floored by it. While plying this chip, it should be done from the hip in a supple fashion, which is far more effective than by striking with the muscles firmly set. Half an hour's practice every day for a month would make any ordinary wrestler almost a proficient in the stroke.

THE CROSS-BUTTOCK.

The cross-buttock and buttock have both been previously described. The only difference. that exists between the Cumberland and Westmorland and the catch-hold "buttocks" is in the hold. In the latter system, one of the best methods is to seize your opponent's left arm or wrist with your right hand, and while you place your left arm round his body, to cross his left leg vigorously with your left, twisting him down the while with a vigorous jerk. The cross-buttock is not difficult to elude, as, when you feel it coming, all you have to do is to secure a tight hold of your opponent's waist, and get in front of him before he accomplishes his object, and his downfall is almost certain, as yours will then be the best position.

The Buttock.

This is similar to the cross-buttock, but it is necessary in the case of the buttock to get your hip further under your

THE HALF-NELSON ON THE GROUND.

man, in order to throw him over your own back without using the legs, as in the cross-buttock.

THE HALF-NELSON.

This is a favourite method with the catch-hold wrestlers of various countries, and a very difficult chip to avoid. As you face your opponent, grasp him by the right wrist with your left hand, then thrust your right hand quickly under his arm, while you firmly seize him by the neck and press his head forward. Your adversary is then completely in your power, as you can quit his right hand, and, by clasping him round the waist, give him the Cornish "heave" (page 27) on to his back. Where ground wrestling is allowed, it is a most effective weapon in the hands of an expert, as the illustration (see page 40) will amply testify. Frequently the wrestler operated upon is thrown a "fair back" on all four points. However, should he happen not to receive a "fair back," as it is called in Devonshire and Cornwall, although he may wriggle for a time, and make a "bridge" (see page 42), as it is termed in Lancashire, ultimately he is compelled to surrender, as nothing can possibly save him.

THE DOUBLE NELSON.

This is very difficult to put in practice, and can only be performed upon a slender individual. To get behind an opponent, put both your arms under his, and clasp your hands behind the back of his head, is not an easy matter in the case of a broad-shouldered man; whereas a comparatively slight exertion on the part of a very big man will enable him to accomplish his object when he has a much

MAKING THE "BRIDGE."

smaller antagonist to deal with. However, as the double nelson is forbidden at most wrestling gatherings in this country, it would serve no useful purpose to make any further remarks on the subject.

CHAPTER V.

SCOTTISH WRESTLING.

BEFORE the Reformation, almost every town and village in Scotland had its great annual meeting for wrestling, tossing the caber, throwing the hammer, etc.; but that great event nearly obliterated everything in the shape of amusement, and probably the whole of the ancient pastimes have not been revived up to the present day. In the Border counties of Scotland, the Cumberland and Westmorland style is practised; but further north, in the neighbourhood of the Bridge of Allan and Stirling, ground wrestling, of a Lancashire style, is now often indulged in at numerous athletic gatherings "ayont the Tweed." Some quarter of a century ago, this system of wrestling was introduced into Scotland by the celebrated Donald Dinnie, who, although a good all-round athlete, was but a poor hand at wrestling on the "first down to lose" principle; but, in his peregrinations round the world, the astute Dinnie no doubt discovered the fact that, owing to his immense strength, he could battle successfully with most men on the ground. Forty years ago, this mode of wrestling was unknown across the Border. Had it existed then, such men as William Jackson, of Kennie-side, Robert Atkinson, the Sleagill giant, Tom Longmire, of Troutbeck, and other champions would assuredly have been in the thick of the fray, as they were at that time the best men in Cumberland and Westmorland. Strictly speaking, Scotchmen do not excel in wrestling, this is probably through want of opportunities to practise the exercise. Only once has a Scotchman taken the all-weight prize at Carlisle, and that was in 1812, when James Scott, of Canonbie, Dumfriesshire, threw all comers in the Cumberland and Westmorland style. Year by year the pastime is becoming more popular, and a certain brawny Scot of the name of Davidson is at the present time holding his own in the catch-hold style, which includes ground wrestling, with the Cumbrian champions, Steadman and Lowden. No one can help thinking, however, that Donald Dinnie would have better served his native land had he introduced a different system.

Without doubt, wrestling was practised on "first down to lose" conditions by the Scottish nobility at an early period, and very little research would prove the fact beyond all dispute. The Ettrick Shepherd, in his description of the contest between Carmichael and Norman Hunter, of Polmood, makes the two champions compete in the Cumberland and Westmorland style. Carmichael was difficult to please in the hold, and caused his opponent to lose his grip three or four times. Finally, when the pair closed, Hunter whipped his opponent up in his arms and threw him like a child. The "Shepherd" had a great opinion of Geordie Cochrane's "heel chip," which he considered invincible when properly plied. Now, in ground wrestling, heel chips are not of much service to a competitor, as the struggle proper does not commence till the men are on all fours.

CHAPTER VI.

FRENCH WRESTLING.

THE visit of the French wrestlers to the Agricultural Hall, in January, 1870, somewhat initiated the British public into the mysterious surroundings of French wrestling. The contest between the French and English champions was distinguished by being universally spoken of as an international match. As the two styles of wrestling were so widely different and so utterly opposed to each other, opinions vary very much as to whether the display deserved to come under the category of an international contest. So-called international contests have been plentiful enough, but few have been deserving of that title, for in most cases it will be found that the so-called foreigners have not only descended from British progenitors, but most of them have actually spoken the same language.

It is well known that foreigners have always been chary of meeting at close quarters the British Lion, and almost the only case recorded of the gauntlet having been thrown down by an alien wrestler was about thirty-five years ago in the ring at Newcastle-on-Tyne, when a renowned champion from France, named Henri, offered to take on all comers, and Richard Wright, of Longtown, John Palmer, of Bewcastle, and John Ivison, of Carlisle, responded. Twenty years later, it was Wright again, along with his famous rival, William Jameson, who promptly replied to the challenge of the French giants, Dubois and Le Bœuf, who were then appearing at the Agricultural Hall, Islington.

On the part of the Englishmen, the match was regarded almost in the light of a joke, and a walk-over was confidently anticipated. Indeed, so sanguine were the two northern champions of victory, that neither of them took the slightest trouble either to get fit for the encounter or to study the tactics of their opponents. Jameson and Wright were then at the head of their profession, and for years had had no rivals. How far they were out in their calculations was soon revealed to them when they had to face the gigantic Frenchmen in the Gallic fashion. Certainly, the Englishmen won in their own style with ease; but they were perfect babies in the hands of their opponents when it came to battling on the ground.

The French rules given below will enable the reader to form some idea of what the Cumbrians had to learn and how much to unlearn before they could possess the remotest chance in coping with their formidable antagonists.

1. The wrestlers are only allowed to take hold from the head, and not lower than the waist.

2. Taking hold of the legs and tripping are strictly forbidden.

3. The wrestling is with open hands, and the wrestlers are not allowed to strike, scratch, or to clasp hands. Clasping hands means that the wrestlers shall not clasp one of their hands within the other, nor interlace their fingers; but they are allowed to grasp their own wrists to tighten their hold round their opponent's body or otherwise.

4. The wrestlers must have their hair cut short, also their finger-nails, and they must wrestle either barefooted or with socks.

5. If one of the wrestlers fall on his knee, shoulder, or side, they have to start again.

6. If the wrestlers roll over each other, the one whose shoulders shall touch the carpet first is deemed conquered.

7. To be conquered, it is necessary that both shoulders of the fallen shall touch the ground at the same time, so as to be fairly seen by the judges and the public.

The match was decided in favour of the Frenchmen, who won the toss for the odd fall, and, naturally enough, chose their own style for the deciding throw. Had the Englishmen won the toss, the result would of course have been reversed. In competing in the French style for the first time, Jameson and Wright were hemmed in by a host of restrictions, and as they were forbidden to trip, they were almost helpless in the hands of their opponents, who in the aggregate weighed five stone odd more than the Englishmen. Yet, notwithstanding this disparity in weight, the Frenchmen did not gain *one fall* in the English style, in which they had been instructed by one of the most skilful English wrestlers, nor could they have succeeded in their own, had the test been which man could bring the other to the ground. A better proof of this could not have been given than in the final fall between Wright and Dubois. The weight of the latter exceeded that of Wright by five and a half stone. Yet the gallant Cumbrian champion hurled his burly antagonist to the ground, and only failed in turning him on his back by not following up his advantage quickly enough. He did the same in his previous encounter with Le Bœuf, whereas, out of the four falls in the Cumberland and Westmorland style, had either Frenchman made the Englishman touch the ground, even with one knee, he would have been entitled to the fall.

A more absurd set of rules than those relating to French wrestling could not well be imagined. In fact, French wrestling, instead of being the art of standing up, is simply the art of getting down on the ground in a certain position. Apart from its roughness, and the danger which attends it, the Lancashire system is certainly superior, as unlimited action is allowed under certain conditions, both as to tripping and clasping the hands. A system that does not teach a man to keep on his legs and retain his perpendicular is of very little service either as an athletic exercise or a means of self-defence. In a hand-to-hand encounter, tripping is the very essence of the art of wrestling; consequently, if that is prohibited, the stronger and heavier man must always have an extra commanding advantage over a lesser opponent, which in English wrestling he does not always possess, as the superior agility of a light-weight exponent of the exercise often makes up for what he is wanting in avoirdupois. As the French style of wrestling or any other form of ground wrestling can never become popular, this division of our subject may be summarily dismissed.

CHAPTER VII.

GERMAN WRESTLING.

THE style of wrestling which finds favour in the land of the Teutons so much resembles the French system that it is scarcely necessary to enter into any detailed description of it further than to state that the numerous restrictions which surround it convey the idea that scarcely anything is allowed to be done while the wrestlers are on their feet. Indeed, a contest in the German fashion is, to all intents and purposes, a struggle on the ground, and a fierce one too, as both shoulders must be squarely held down before a decision is given. As in French wrestling, tripping, back-heeling, and clicking are forbidden, and as you must not turn your back to your opponent, neither the buttock nor cross-buttock can come into operation; consequently, nothing remains but strength and stamina to battle with. When the wrestlers come to close quarters, the principal object seems to be to get the under-hold, *i.e.*, to get both arms round the waist and under the armpits, so as to lift the adversary off the ground and swing him on to his back.

With men of equal size it is almost impossible to obtain a throw with one arm above and one underneath, as in the Cumberland and Westmorland fashion, without using the feet to hipe, cross-buttock, inside click, or strike on the outside. The wrestlers are forbidden to catch hold of the legs, or, indeed, to touch below the waist. To have first to throw your man down without tripping him, and afterwards battle with him on the ground on all fours, until one or the other is compelled to give in through sheer exhaustion, is a style of wrestling utterly opposed to our insular notions of fair-play, and although the system finds favour in Lancashire and in certain parts of Scotland, it will never take rank as the recognized style of wrestling in this country.

CHAPTER VIII.

JAPANESE WRESTLING.

WRESTLING holds a high position among athletic exercises in Japan, and in the encouragement of this ancient exercise by such an intelligent people, something more than mere pastime is kept in view. Probably, in imitation of the ancient Greeks and Romans, these exercises are considered a kind of preparation for the battle of life, or even the exigencies of war. Their wrestling contests are sometimes held in enclosed buildings, and frequently in booths, but generally speaking in the open air, in a ring surrounded by a railing about three feet high. The Japanese wrestlers are a most formidable class of men, being usually immensely stout, and when adorned in their war-paint, with a huge belt round the waist, and their enormous calves encased in stout leggings, their appearance is enough to strike terror even to the beholder, not to mention the opponent who gazes on the giants for the first time. A contest in Japan creates the greatest excitement among the spectators, who cheer their favourites after the recognized European fashion. At the

E

conclusion of a public competition, each victor presents himself to the judge, who, as a rule, awards a silver or gold plate, bearing the imperial arms. In recent years, however, as the exercise has become extremely popular, more substantial rewards have been given.

The most celebrated Japanese wrestler of the present day is named Matsada Sorakichi, who, when he was touring in America, offered £10 to any athlete who could stand before him and remain unthrown for twenty minutes. It is said the "Jap" made money by these challenges; but he was almost frightened out of his wits when he was introduced to Evan Lewis, *alias* "The Strangler." When Matsada ascertained who his opponent was, he promptly refused to meet Lewis, who is only a little over twelve stone in weight. "The Strangler" is a wonderful wrestler, and throws his men with the "grape-vine," a method closely resembling the Cumberland "hank."

ADDENDA.

In conclusion, the following queries recently received may be replied to here without being out of place :—

Q. What are the duties of a referee ?

A. The referee's duties are to get the wrestlers together and give his decision when the umpires disagree. His verdict is final ; as he is supposed to be a competent person, no one can interfere.

Q. What constitutes a fall in the Græco-Roman style ?

A. Two shoulders on the ground. The same applies to French wrestling, for which Græco-Roman is merely another name.

Q. What constitutes a fall in the Cornwall and Devon style ?

A. Two shoulders and one hip, or two hips and one shoulder ; it makes no difference which it is. But in a "four-point" match, a man must be thrown on both shoulders and both hips before any other portion of his body touches the ground ere a verdict is recorded against him.

Q. What constitutes a fall in the Cumberland and Westmorland style ?

A. Any portion of the body on the ground, hand or knee, or quitting hold before the throw is made.

Q. What constitutes a fall in the Lancashire style ?

A. Struggling on the ground is the principal feature in

Lancashire wrestling, and two shoulders down constitute a fall.

Q. Should a man make a "bridge" in Lancashire wrestling, from head to heel, is it unfair to press him with the elbow or otherwise cause him pain?

A. It is unfair to injure an opponent in any tender part of the body, and throttling is not allowed, yet frequently indulged in. Although throttling is forbidden, a wrestler may put his arm tightly round his opponent's neck and cause him excessive pain.

Q. Would you bar the "double nelson?"

A. Certainly the "double nelson" should be barred, as being both dangerous and brutal.

Q. Should ground wrestling be abolished?

A. Ground wrestling, in the opinion of most people qualified to discuss the subject, ought never to have been introduced into this country, as it is decidedly un-English, and calculated to bring an ancient pastime into disrepute.

There can be no objection to the catch-hold system, "first down to lose" the fall, to catch hold above the waist without being restricted to any particular grip. In a "first down to lose" contest, the referee has not the same difficulty in giving a decision which he must experience in all "three-point" matches.

Unquestionably, if an amalgamated style of wrestling were introduced throughout the country, the ancient science of wrestling would assume its proper position among the numerous athletic exercises for which this land of vigorous and manly outdoor sports is so justly famous.

www.ingramcontent.com/pod-product-compliance
Lightning Source LLC
Chambersburg PA
CBHW022022080426
42733CB00007B/692